LOVE TOUCHDOWN

A MARRIAGE PLAYBOOK

THOMAS & PATRICE
HENDERSON

LTD Publishing

Order additional copies of this book from
Amazon.com.

Contact info:
mrdcpls@yahoo.com
630-200-8090

This book is dedicated to two "till death do us part" couples, our parents:

Reverend Morris Sr. & Dr. Eva J Purnell
(65 Years)

And

Joseph II & Evelyn Henderson
(46 Years)

Thank you for providing us a glimpse into the realities of long-term marriage.

To our legacy children: Nicole, Bryon & Ricky

To our legacy grandchildren: Andrew, Aidan, Madison, Xavier, Yara and Zamir

ACKNOWLEDGEMENTS

To our pastor and first lady, James T & Jamell Meeks, for recognizing God's gift in us as a couple and trusting us to lead and teach other married couples.

To Thomas & Stephanie Morish, for inspiring us with the theme for this book.

To Yvette, Beth, Brenda & Kim for their constant encouragement to complete the book.

To Andre & Ginaya Hampton – Photo "Special Request Entertainment" & Make-up "Faces By Hollywood".

To Dr. Stanley Robertson, for leading us down the path to have this book become a reality.

To the Salem Marriage Ministry, who have graciously served under our leadership to reach other couples through fun activities, facilitating educational sessions, and offering a shoulder to lean on.

To the thousands of couples who we believe have benefited from our teaching and have entrusted us to coach, mentor, partner, and encourage them through their own playbook of love.

CONTENTS

LOVE TOUCHDOWN

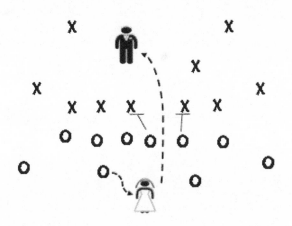

FOREWORD

For more than 40 years, Thomas and Patrice Henderson have been an integral part of our lives, and have left an indelible impact on our church family. They have influenced discipleship, supported the growth of our church, and helped us reach hurting families beyond our four walls. As a couple, I consider them to be an authority on healthy, biblical marriage.

I have trusted them to strengthen the marriages of our church through biblical teaching, coaching and support. I've watched them counsel and encourage couples, walking them through all types of challenges and helping them to grow in their marriage. Through retreats, classes, workshops and training they have built an amazing marriage ministry in our church, and have birthed marriage ministries around the world.

The words contained in this book shares the practical wisdom, insights and hope that their ministry has provided to thousands of couples. I'm grateful that they have taken everything they have poured out from their many years of fruitful leadership, and captured them on these pages. I'm confident that this book will help couples as well as marriage leaders gain the understanding needed to inspire greater faithfulness in marriage.

Pastor James T. Meeks, Senior Pastor
Salem Baptist Church of Chicago, Inc.

INTRODUCTION

Does your spouse look forward to spending more time watching football than he does with you? Does your spouse regularly silence your family in the middle of a big play, or does his mood change based on whether his team wins or loses? Some men are obsessed with football, and it is slowly ruining their marriages. It can consume their lives and is virtually guaranteed to occupy all of their time every football season.

If you are just as passionate about football as your spouse is, then you're in luck. However, this is a rarity since most women know little about the game. In *Love Touch Down*, we will help you increase your knowledge of this passionate American sport, while at the same time giving you tips on how to energize your marriage. Throughout this playbook, you will see many similarities between marriage and the game of football. So, while you are learning more about marriage, you will be picking up tips that will help you develop a deeper level of companionship with your spouse and drawing closer to him than you ever dreamed possible.

The book is divided into six sections that will increase your marital bliss, while at the same time allowing you to understand the game of football and its similarities to marriage. This book will also help you accept your husband's fanaticism, and it may even help you appreciate his most favored pastime.

Prologue: The Draft Process

The first section of *Love Touch Down* is devoted to the draft process. In football, the draft is where a team vets and selects a player who is a right fit for that team. This section of *Love Touch Down* provides a general overview of how one goes through a similar process of vetting when dating or planning for a long-term relationship. This period in a relationship should be an important screening process for long-term success and should not be solely based upon external features or fleeting emotions.

First Quarter: The Kickoff

The game of football begins with the kickoff. In marriage, the relationship is kicked off with the official wedding ceremony. The wedding signifies the beginning of your life together, with what hopes to be a winning season of eternal bliss. In *Love Touch Down*, this section discusses the minor transitions that are made by each spouse to adjust to each other's lifestyle, values, and habits. The kickoff period will help to fine-tune those things that work and expose those that were not readily discovered during the initial draft process.

Second Quarter: The Honeymoon Is Over

This is the point in the relationship where reality sets in, but there should be no options to punt or forfeit the game. In this section, we give you tips on how to adjust to a new set of rules. We also give you insights for determining who should be the referee to mediate those issues that may have been glossed over during the two previous periods.

Halftime: Reviewing the First Half

In football, halftime is a long break that happens between the second and third quarters. This allows the players and their team enough time to reorganize and make necessary adjustments for the second half of the game. Your marriage may benefit from this same sort of analysis. Things may not be going exactly the way you planned, or they may be sailing along at a nice pace, but a review of the strategy for the long-term win is warranted. In this section of *Love Touch Down,* we explore any unfair calls that may have happened during the first half and help you learn how to score in the relationship.

Third Quarter: Reworking the Offense and the Defense

At this point in your relationship, you may have faced some serious challenges. If this is the case, it may require the use of sideline coaches and counselors who can provide objective feedback and help you effectively analyze the next play. Now that two quarters have been played, it is imperative to have an understanding of the external influences that might negatively impact your marriage. It is important to know how to have a good defense to ward off detractors, as well as a healthy offense to keep things moving forward.

Fourth Quarter: Winning the Game

In football, the referee stops the game when there are two minutes left at the end of each half. This is referred to as the two-minute warning. It is often one of the most exciting parts of a football game. It is a crucial point in the game because it gives each team a chance to execute a series of plays that could change the game's outcome. During the two-minute warning, each team has time to gather to discuss their strategy. Years into your marriage, you may also need some time to regroup and strategize. Because of the challenges a relationship might face over the years, this is a time where the best strategies must be engaged and could possibly alter the outcome of hurt feelings. In this section, we discuss divorce, compromises, and commitments and give you plays on how to win the game.

PROLOGUE
The Draft Process

I could hear the roar of his home theater system in the man cave, but my concentration was on quietly descending the carpeted stairs in my four-inch heels. I had never attempted to do something like this before, but one thing was for sure: I wanted my man, and I was positive that he wanted me. As I made my way down the last three treads of the stairway, I could see that he was slumped down on the couch in his boxers, so seducing and conquering was going to be easier than I had expected. I called his name ever so softly, just above a whisper, so that he would purposely have to turn around to behold the silhouette of his beloved. He didn't turn around, so I raised the volume of my voice just moderately, enough to be heard over the TV, but this time I called him by his pet name. He knows that when he's called by that name it's for a special, flirty reason. On the last stair step, I was now about seven feet from him. For some reason, he still didn't turn around, so without paying attention to what was playing on the television, I fondled his hair in a playful way, without allowing him to see me fully, while standing behind the couch. He gently pushed my hand away and said, "Honey, can't it wait for an hour or two?"

Stiletto Heels and Victoria's Secret

So there I was, all dressed up in my special little outfit. I knew that we had not been intimate within the last two weeks, so I figured there was no way that he was going to turn me down. I was dressed in his favorite lingerie. It was the negligee that he had purchased for me from Victoria's Secret for our anniversary the prior year, and also stiletto heels, which he goes crazy about when he sees other women in them. He had grabbed a good nap and had gotten home by 7:00 that morning. He had already gotten some sleep, so I knew he would be in the mood, and I was definitely already there. This was going to be a special time for the two of us, especially for him. His favorite perfume scent is Angel, so I made sure to put it on in the right places, where I would be able to captivate his attention. I planned this oh-so-perfectly, as I knew that he would be settled in his favorite spot on the downstairs sofa in front of his newly purchased 70-inch big screen TV.

Determined not to be discouraged by whatever had captured his attention, I decided to come around in front of him in my sultry outfit. I playfully sat on his lap and whispered in his ear. "Bobby," I said, "I've got a surprise for you."

Without moving his eyes from television, he said, "Hey babe, can't it just wait for a little while? Don't you know that Sunday football has just started?"

I immediately jumped off of his lap and shouted, "*Sunday football!* Aren't you more interested in playing games with me?"

He said, "Sure babe, let's just wait until halftime." It made me wonder, *Was my husband getting a booty call elsewhere?*

Was the football game about to be my competition? It didn't have blond hair, brunette hair, or a small curvy waist and firm backside. It was just a stupid game, foiling the obvious pass I was trying to make on my man. Just like the personal foul in football, your marriage will suffer a stiff penalty for cheating, and it certainly can be risky to the cheater's health.

I didn't have the first clue as to why he was so fascinated with football. I had never dated anyone in school who played football. Basketball? Yes, but not football. What was so intriguing about this stupid game that the smell of a voluptuous woman wouldn't be able to tear him away from it? And what is halftime, anyway? I don't like football, but I guess if this "babe" was going to be my new competition, then I had better get to know who my competition was and make sure that I could use her to get my man back.

Heather's Story

That was Heather's story (not her real name). One day she came into my office, crying her eyes out, and said that she wanted to talk woman-to-woman, as she was seriously considering leaving her husband because he seemed to put other things above her. She felt that she was being cheated in the love that she felt was due her. Her story was what led to writing this book.

My husband and I have been married for over 40 years. Though many would boast about the number of years, they would also boast that their marriage has been filled with marital bliss. We, like other couples, struggled for many years to get on a common page, move in the same direction, and even just consistently like each other. We have been fortunate to speak to hundreds of couples over the past 35 years and felt compelled to share reflective successes of how they were able to move past and through critical moments in their relationships.

In football, a **personal foul** is an illegal, flagrant foul considered risky to the health of another player. This type of foul carries one of the stiffest penalties in the game of football. The same is true in marriage with a spouse who cheats. There are few things worse than a cheating husband, and one of the signs of infidelity is when the sexual attraction fades.

An older woman once gave me this piece of advice: "Never let your competition know that you fear her. Always show or display that you are confident and that your marriage is on a solid foundation. This will cause her to wonder and question, Are you a secure or stupid wife? This will surely cause her to lose her footing and keep her questioning her own skills and abilities and eventually give up when there is no longer a sense of insecurity on your part."

Football was so important to Heather's husband that he was willing to sacrifice the sexual pleasures of erotic lovemaking with his wife! He enjoyed it that much.

Through that experience, Heather recognized that, for men, marriage is much like a game of football. If she had the skill and stamina to navigate the relationship, her marriage could go the distance. But dirty tackles and trick plays would almost always get her sent off for an early bath!

The Football Draft

Football! It's considered to be one of America's most passionate pastimes. It is a game that is full of action from beginning to end, and it can have its nail-biting moments as each quarter ends, especially once the two-minute warning is sounded. The financial implications of the game are staggering. Games can draw an average of 60,000 people and generate billions of dollars each year. Half the stadiums are filled with orange t-shirts and the other half with green. The people with the orange t-shirts dislike the people with the green ones, even though they otherwise have nothing in common. This bizarre and extreme die-hard behavior is fanaticism at best!

For many die-hard fans, draft day is the highlight of the season because it is the time where each team has their choice of the eligible players. This event goes on for days and is often viewed by millions of people.

I learned that the team's owners use a term known as "vetting" to look at prospective players. It derives from the same term used in veterinary science. It is attributed to the practice of verifying the condition of a racehorse to determine its fitness prior to engaging it in a race. It's a fine-tooth medical review process to assure that the animal can endure a grueling race. Since a significant financial investment is being made in a potential player, this rigorous testing process is intense, as it will analyze the player from a physical, emotional, psychological, and social perspective.

After the draft process is complete, the selected players gear up for training camp. For those who are new to the team, this can be an ideal time to acclimate to the environment of the coaching staff and other players. All of the players get to learn the moods of their respective teammates, but, more importantly, they learn techniques that will help them work cohesively as a team, so that their winning synergy can be rhythmic in nature and their souls meshed, like brothers, to form a bond that will lead to a victorious season.

Couples go through this same sort of draft process before they get married. In the relationship, the draft is a period where each person evaluates the other and tries to make a determination of whether they are right for each other. After learning a little more about football from my husband, I realized that, like football, marriage is an investment that demands full consideration, as well as understanding the potential cost of such an investment and whether it is wise to enter into. It also made me realize that the draft phase should not be taken lightly. It is the best time to learn and apply some successful principles to give yourself the best chance to have a winning marriage.

The draft phase of a relationship is about getting to know each other to determine if the two of you may be a good fit for a long-term connection. It is advisable not to rush the dating portion of the relationship since this is a time where you can understand if you are compatible with your potential mate. One of the benefits of dating before marriage is that you have no responsibilities to fulfill; all you have to do is get to know each other. This is a great time to find out about the other person's likes and dislikes. You will also be able to learn about your partner's quirks and idiosyncrasies and understand what annoys him. When you begin the dating process, there may be an endless amount of things to talk about; however, as your relationship grows older, you may want to discuss more meaningful topics to help you evaluate whether the two of you are headed toward a positive, healthy relationship. Here is a list of some of the things you can talk about to help you vet your potential mate and get your relationship off to a running start.

- **Your expectations.** Everyone has expectations for their relationships, but what you expect and what your partner expects are not necessarily the same. Getting one's needs met is one of the key ingredients to a healthy relationship; therefore, it is extremely important for each person to understand what the other expects in a marriage. Those expectations are shaped by one's family background, prior relationships, and/or other external factors.

- **Your spiritual beliefs.** Your spiritual beliefs will affect the quality of your marriage. Most people are very passionate when it comes to religion. A lack of understanding of your spouse's faith can be a major cause of frustration. When having these discussions, be sure to listen to your partner and avoid being judgmental.

- **Your family.** Family is one of the prime areas of debate in a marriage. Your family can have a positive or negative impact on your relationship, so it is critical to be transparent about your parents, siblings, and other relatives. You should let your partner know if there are any serious medical issues in your family history that may be hereditary. It is also a good thing to discuss how close you are to your family or any estrangements.

- **Your personal goals.** Your dreams and aspirations are of vital importance to your spouse. This may include a discussion of things such as whether you will have children, and if so, then how many. We have seen many relationships fractured because assumptions were made or fears were not disclosed. You might also discuss where you want to live, whether you want to hyphenate or even take on your spouse's last name, and, most important, your views on sex.

- **Your financial goals.** Perhaps one of the most contentious areas in any marriage relates to finances. You should have an open and honest discussion about your financial goals, as well as your current financial position. This is especially true if you have bad credit or a large amount of outstanding debt due to school loans, child support, or alimony.

The football draft gives each team the opportunity to infuse their roster with new talent. But the best teams are not looking for a player to complete them; instead, they are looking for a player who adds value to the franchise. In order to get drafted, a player must not only be a good football player on the field, they must also make the team look good off the field as well.

During the draft phase of your relationship, you will be looking for a person to be added to your team. This person must be ready to enter the game of marriage and the two of you can conquer the world together.

When considering a potential spouse, you should have a list of criteria that defines what you are looking for in a long-term relationship. If you connect with a person who does not meet your criteria, it may be a good idea to rethink the relationship.

But when you score a love touchdown and connect with that one person with whom you want to spend the rest of your life, it's time for your offensive drive to kick into gear.

Love, Lust, Loneliness & the Offensive Drive

In a marriage, an offensive drive refers to the power or energy that moves the relationship forward. Something very similar happens in football. An offensive drive in football refers to the series of plays a team executes while they are in possession of the ball, and the amount of time it takes to execute those plays.

Ultimately, a drive consists of a series of downs. You may hear this referred to as first down, second down, third down, or fourth down. Whenever a team has control of the ball, they have four plays to advance the ball 10 yards. A down is synonymous with a play, so it simply means that the team in possession of the ball can run four plays to try to gain 10 yards. If they advance the ball 10 yards, they will receive another four downs. If they don't gain 10 yards in four plays, the other team gets the ball and tries to advance it in the opposite direction. The primary goal of a drive is to advance down the field and get the ball into the end zone to score a touchdown.

Just as an offensive drive in football is used to advance a team forward, an offensive drive in your marriage is something that moves the relationship forward. One of the greatest driving forces in your marriage is your emotions, which can have a significant impact in finding the right person with whom to share the rest of your life. Three emotions in particular, love, lust, and loneliness, if not understood, are powerful emotions that can derail your intentions and drive your relationship into the ground.

The words "I love you" are often uttered when there has been a culmination in a physical relationship. The word "love" is very weighty and packs a lot behind it, as with this phrase comes an immediate expectation from the one saying it, and also upon the one hearing it. If this word, "love," were ever put on the periodic table of elements, it could possibly outweigh the atomic particle Copernicium. "I love you" is never a phrase that should be casually stated, as one of the things that both men and women pine for is love. It is sandwiched on Maslow's Hierarchy of Needs, but is the base upon which esteem and self-actualization rest.

Lust is one of those demons that trick us into believing that we care for a person, or that a person cares for us. I'm not speaking of lust in the same context as a person having affection toward someone, but rather the active physical craving that is stimulated by either the thought of being with someone sexually or forfeiting everything or everyone to ensure that a sexual tryst takes place. There are no fingers being pointed here, for I too live in a glass house and know that sexuality is a powerful animal and can be ferocious if not tamed. It literally breaks my heart to hear how both men and women often feel abandoned as soon as they want to stop or slow down their sexual encounters. One of the first questions that I ask those people is, "How long did you know them before you engaged in a sexual relationship with them?" The answer is not surprising but often disheartening, as most times it was the first or second date.

Loneliness is the hardest of all. When a person confesses to being lonely, they are usually saying that no one loves them, and the same way that it was referred to with Maslow, their esteem and self-actualization cannot be manifested because this void has yet to be filled. It is my personal belief that being alone is not the same as being lonely. I can be in a room full of people, yet feel that no one in the room notices me or cares about me, and thus a great sense of desperation rushes in, attempting to fill that chasm of loneliness with anyone who will satisfy my time and space. On the other hand, if my confidence has not been shaken, and I really like who I am, and I don't feel as though it takes someone else to complete me, then being alone can be a very good place to be. Many people take time alone to read a book, watch a program on television, or jog along a lake or riverfront and are as content pg. as they can be, because they are not lonely and don't need to seek predators who will swoop down and prey upon soul and emotions.

It is not always easy to determine what the motive of another person is, and this is not an indictment upon anyone who attempts to truly love someone who has been lonely. It is an indictment upon the one who takes advantage of someone's heart, someone's resources, with no intent of giving back. It is better to be alone than in a relationship with someone who makes you feel lonely.

That's what the draft phase of the relationship is all about. It is important to get to know the other person before you jump into a long-term commitment like marriage. Just like the draft in football, you should use this time wisely before making a selection decision because whoever you choose, the two of you will have special rights to each other to the exclusion of all others. Take your time and find out what the other person likes and dislikes. It may take some time to break through the plastic mask of the masquerade, but it is worth it.

MARRIAGE PLAYBOOK
COACHING STRATEGY
Prologue: The Draft Process

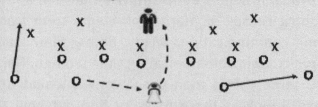

- Take your time to get to know a potential mate. Whether they were introduced to you by a friend or you were connected by a dating website, slow the process down to temper the emotions, and never neglect the logical or the glaring warning signs.

- Spend time around your mate's family. Yes, you are marrying their family as well. Don't get caught up in the trap that you are the only one in their life that should matter. Carefully observe how they treat their family members. Do they care for or neglect them?

- Commit up to ¼ of the dollars you will spend on a wedding to secure pre-marital counseling.

Your Love Touchdown Playlist

It probably comes as no surprise that one of the leading causes of marital problems stem from poor communication. Many times, men have more trouble communicating than women. Here are some things men wish women would do. Take a look at these plays to find out how to love him and how to make him happy; then place a checkmark next to one of the plays that you will commit to making today.

- Compliment him to his face.

- Learn to prepare his favorite meal.

- Let him overhear you compliment him to others.

- Listen to his dreams.

- Write him a love letter.

- Marvel at his talents.

2 minute wrap-up

What are some of the key points that you have learned from this section?

_____

_____

_____

What type of playbook strategy would you develop to improve or keep your relationship consistent?

_____

_____

_____

If you were providing advice to a friend based on what you read in this section, what would be the one key takeaway?

_____

_____

_____

FIRST QUARTER
The Kickoff

Every football game begins with a kickoff. This is usually preceded by a coin toss made by the referee, and the team that calls the flip of the coin correctly gets to decide whether they wish to kick or receive the ball. In most cases, the team that won the coin toss usually wants to receive the ball so they can take advantage of the first offensive possession. There could be a significant advantage for this, especially since all the players are fresh to the game, and the other team hasn't quite figured out what some of their moves might be. There have even been some historical plays whereby the team that receives the kickoff has been able to run the ball all the way down the field for a touchdown in the beginning minutes of the game. Imagine what type of energy goes up in a stadium when, in the first few minutes of the game, a team has been able to put the first points up on the board! Devin Hester, a wide receiver for the Chicago Bears, did complete such a play in Super Bowl XLI against the Indianapolis Colts, running an amazing 92 yards for such a touchdown. In fact, this was the eighth time in Super Bowl history that this type of play had occurred. I can remember my husband and I (both from Chicago) leaping out of our seats in disbelief at how such a young rookie would be able to pull off such a thing in the game of games, the Super Bowl.

When I think about this in the context of marriage, this is how every marriage starts off. Whether you had your ceremony performed at the justice of the peace, city hall, in a large cathedral or church, or at your home on a well-manicured lawn, this became the official moment in which your relationship became a marriage, and the two of you were now attempting to become one. Depending on what culture you come from, I've seen people break glasses, jump brooms, run through a rainy shower of rice pellets, or gracefully move down an aisle of white plastic, anxious to start their lives together. They can never be sure of what their future holds for them, but at that moment in time, they believe that they can conquer the world against all of its odds, and truthfully, that is the way they should start. They should never assume that things are not going to work out.

Winning Attitudes Win

Football players never go into a game thinking that they are going to lose. There are betting parlors all over America that establish odds for and against teams, so unless a game is expected to be thrown, a coach always goes in with a winning attitude, feeling that he can surmount the challenges of perhaps a stronger team. In marriage, sometimes the stronger team seems to be the opposition or the forces that are present at the time that the couple says, "I do." Those forces are sometimes individuals who prayed that this union would never take place, either for their own personal gain or because they feared that it was not in the best interest of both parties. Regardless of the external factors, the couple usually forges ahead on their special day, believing that the best is yet to come.

Long before the actual wedding takes place, there is a lengthy to-do list that is usually penned by the bride-to-be. She wants this day to represent the most perfect of days, and almost all young girls have dreamed of this day since they were old enough to understand what marriage meant. Growing up as a young girl, I envisioned the perfect wedding ceremony, but since that was so long ago, it was not as elaborate as those that I see today. Most young girls fantasize about that special day, and even act the ceremony out at times, participating in events known as "Tom Thumb" weddings. For me, the most important aspect of wedding day was being sure that the church would be packed with friends and loved ones and that all eyes would focus on me as I marched slowly down the aisle in a pristine white dress, with a glorious veil to match. My prince in shining armor would be poised at the altar, waiting to take my hand as we began our blissful lives together. Since this day had to be the most special of all, the right church, the right music, the right wedding party, and most definitely the right wedding invitation all had to be in order to assure that this day would be the wedding of all weddings, but particularly that it would be the epitome of a young girl's anticipation of finally becoming the bride.

By what may seem like gossip that spreads like wildfire, wedding planners learn of pending nuptials and want to place their bids to assure that each wedding day will be a memorable day for the Prince Charming and his bride. It is highly recommended that couples sit down and talk with the minister or officiant who would marry them, not out of formality but as a necessity.

For most brides-to-be, the hours seem to be endless, as each new day marks that they are getting close to the actual wedding date. Another important aspect is the planning of the honeymoon. The bride definitely must have input, so that she can boast about how far they traveled, how many sites they saw, how many excursions they went on, how many selfies they took, and last but not least, how many romantic encounters they had during their glorious honeymoon adventure. For her, this is a dream come true, and for him, it's not something he has dreamed about all of his life, but it is something that he is definitely happy to be a part of.

The ceremony itself is one of the most beautiful days that any woman would ever imagine. This day will be etched in their memories, on Instagram, Facebook, and other social media, as well as in elaborate video productions, capturing the tender and fun moments that they were too emotionally caught up to see. Friends, family, and loved ones are present, as well as the wedding crasher, who doesn't know the bride, groom, or any of the related guests, but is just looking for a good time. The day is punctuated with laughter, frivolity, and cheers of celebration for the lucky couple. It is the belief of most of the attendees that not only do the newlyweds look great together as a couple, but they also look like they belong together.

The wedding reception is just as important in the planning process (which is typically an expensive venture). It is a culminating event to celebrate to the nuptial of the couple as they joyfully stuff cake into each other's faces, dance the mandatory first dance, and waltzes into a longer day of receiving their guests, who are there to shower them with their best wishes and gifts.

All of this can sometimes lead to a fairy tale concept of marriage that can be problematic when real life sets in. Since real life is not a fairy tale, it is important not to romanticize your marriage like it's a Lifetime movie, and one of the first things you should recognize in order to keep your marriage based in reality is that your spouse is not going to complete you.

Quarterback and Wide Receiver Connections

Two people may seem to complete each other on the football turf, but that is not so common in marriage. Take the quarterback and the wide receiver as an example. These are two of the most exciting positions in the game of football. They have a symbiotic relationship because they need each other to do what they do, which, together, is score touchdowns. The quarterback is usually the leader of the team and is responsible for calling the plays in the huddle. Wide receivers are offensive players who specialize in catching passes from the quarterback. Quarterbacks and wide receivers can make spectacular plays when a skilled quarterback throws the ball past every player on the field and delivers it exactly where it needs to go, like threading a needle. These types of connections make it easy to see why the symbiotic relationship between a quarterback and wide receiver is so important. They need each other to complete the play and get the ball into the end zone for the touchdown.

Finding Meaningful Connections

As a couple, we believe that it is an impractical theory to suggest that couples complete each other, but couples should be in the habit of establishing meaningful connections. My husband and I had an early morning TV ritual. I used to get up and watch shows like *Law and Order* or *CSI*. My husband kept complaining that he was tired of waking up to the morbid darkness of these shows, and he would often become paranoid that I was planning something quite sinister. I agreed that this was probably not the best way for me to start off my mornings, and one day, my husband was in the kitchen laughing so hard that I slowly strolled into the kitchen to find out what had tickled him so much. Both of us love creative comedies, and the more we watch them, the more we get hooked. We stumbled upon a common show that provided us with mutual enjoyment. For some strange reason, we became voyeurs of court TV. I haven't quite figured out why I have become so mesmerized by those shows, as they are representations of the lives of real people, and most have a great focus on the state of domestic situations. Sometimes I am overwhelmed by the fact that people have chosen to put their personal business (often embarrassing situations) on public display. They are not ashamed to talk about the sordid affairs that they have been involved in, or how they deceived their partners into believing that they are someone they are not. After going through the reading of the respective briefs in each case, and after each judge hears further details of what has been happening in these people's lives, it usually boils down to one question that is asked by the judge: "Didn't you know that she/he was this way before you married her/him?" Most of the times, the response is an unequivocal "yes," as the person simply hangs their head in shame that they should have known better and should have followed their first instinct to walk away from such a toxic relationship. Sometimes that person had premonitions, dreams, or even nightmares about staying with that person, but instead, they pressed ahead simply because they were too fearful to face the taunts of those who could see the obvious. In my opinion, when the signs to flee are clear, then don't run like a contestant in the Boston marathon—move like an experienced sprinter. Keep your eye focused on the finish line and don't look back, or else you will be swallowed up by your own lack of self-esteem or the desperate need to feel wanted.

Wives Are Not Jelly Donuts

This conjures the notion that is portrayed in romantic comedies and television shows when a passionate love scene has one of the two people blurt out the phrase, "You complete me." This connotes a visual to me, that as humans, we must be donuts with a large, gaping hole, lacking our jelly filling until we meet our future partners, or that we are fractured pieces of pottery, waiting for the other person (the glue) to put us back together again to make us whole. This is such a flawed concept that people have come to accept or believe, and it is romanticized in such a way that it sounds like it should be right, but creates false expectations. I'm not sure where this concept came from, but probably dates back to the time of Adam and Eve, where in Genesis 2:21–24 (KJV), it is stated as follows:

And the LORD God caused a deep sleep to fall upon Adam, and he slept: and he took one of his ribs, and closed up the flesh instead thereof:

And the rib, which the LORD God had taken from man, made he a woman, and brought her unto the man.

And Adam said, This is now bone of my bones, and flesh of my flesh: she shall be called Woman, because she was taken out of Man.

Therefore shall a man leave his father and his mother, and shall cleave unto his wife: and they shall be one flesh.

If you profess Christianity or are knowledgeable about the Bible, you are aware that God did not want Adam to be alone, so he created Eve for Adam to have as a helpmate. Adam and Eve were both now responsible for human procreation and care of the earth.

Those "you complete me" statements tend to placate one's partner, assuring them that their world would not be complete unless their partner was a part of it. When this is reinforced by committed actions, especially when one is dating seriously, this phrase can have significant value if it is not wasted on an emotional moment, but one where one's partner is attempting to express their long-term intent.

We recently taught a lesson to couples about this completeness theory and helped them to understand that if our self-worth is tied to another individual to make us whole, that same sense of self-worth is at risk if that person is no longer present. As best as possible, individual partners should come into a relationship with a healthy awareness of who they are. If they know their strengths, as well as their own faults, then the search for a mate is not for someone who erases their imperfections, but rather complements them.

While a symbiotic relationship between some players in football may be beneficial, this is not the case in a marriage since it means that one spouse's psychological needs are reliant on the other spouse. This type of codependency could be harmful to each of the individuals in the relationship. A much better approach is a synergistic marriage where the contributions of each spouse can enhance an otherwise healthy spouse's needs in a positive manner.

MARRIAGE PLAYBOOK
COACHING STRATEGY
First Quarter: The Kickoff

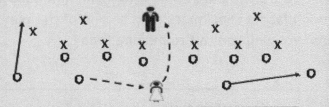

- Don't let the toothpaste tube or toilet seat be the beginning of disaster. Adjusting to each other's habits will take time.

- Be careful not to compare your relationship to that of others. What you see on the outside may not be a true indicator of what's happening on the inside.

- Focus on the goals the two of you chatted about on endless nights prior to marriage. Pick two of them and make a game plan to bring them to reality.

- Keep up the pleasantries that made your relationship special from the beginning. Regular date nights, visiting a favorite restaurant, saying "thank you" and "please." Whatever it took to land your spouse, it will usually take double that to keep them.

Your Love Touchdown Playlist

Take a look at these plays to find out how to love your husband and how to make him happy; then place a checkmark next to one of the plays that you will commit to making today.

- Kiss him at unexpected times.
- Apologize for something you did.
- Thank him for being a great dad.
- Leave a quick message for him to find.
- Ask him what he would like to do.
- Watch a game with him.
- Eat dinner together.

2 minute wrap-up

What are some of the key points that you have learned from this section?

_____

_____

_____

What type of playbook strategy would you develop to improve or keep your relationship consistent?

_____

_____

_____

If you were providing advice to a friend based on what you read in this section, what would be the one key takeaway?

_____

_____

_____

SECOND QUARTER
The Honeymoon Is Over

Ah! The honeymoon! This is the blissful excursion a couple plans to officially consummate their marriage as they begin their trek together as a couple, traveling a road of endless love and fulfilled expectations. We all know that feeling of euphoria. It is wished for, planned for, and saved for, and often we feel envy when couples joyfully announce that they will spend their time in tropical settings with tent-like cabanas nestled on stilts rising out of crystal blue waters, capturing moonlit beams as they sip champagne in specially designed flutes etched with their new initials. It is during this 7–14 days of shared time that they learn of each other's dreams and fears and comfort each other in the promise that they will always be there for each other, encouraging each other and committing to help each other realize their dreams. After they frolic along the white sandy beaches, looking into each other's eyes while riding horses bareback, they rush back to the honeymoon suite to feed each other slices of sumptuous fresh fruit that has been handpicked for their enjoyment.

This romantic location exclusive attention to each other was designed to be a time in which a couple could spend solitary time as they began their life together, especially since they had just experienced a whirlwind ceremony where privacy and intimacy were limited.

It is believed that the word "honeymoon" came from the French phrase *lune de miel*, figuratively meaning "the month of honey." This was to be a celebrated time for couples, as their friends and loved ones would provide them with honey wine, which could be characterized as a mild intoxicant but was potent enough to ensure them happiness and fertility. The Bible has also been credited with giving us a first account of the concept of the honeymoon, which comes from the passage Deuteronomy 24:5, which says, "When a man hath taken a new wife, he shall not go out to war, neither shall he be charged with any business: but he shall be free at home one year, and shall cheer up his wife which he hath taken." Hey guys, could you imagine being commanded to spend one whole year with your new spouse before returning to work? Ladies, would this be seen as a blessing or a curse? LOL.

Conflict Is Inevitable

Then it happens: From out of nowhere, there's a shift in the atmosphere. A quiet storm seems to be approaching on the horizon, when it had seemed as though the sun would beam on the happy couple the entire trip. Something has caused this serene environment to be shattered, as they both discover that they don't agree on the same things, as one prefers to go to the steakhouse, while the other, the seafood buffet. The way that they had once finished each other's sentences in the dating phase, which had been their sign of destiny that they were meant for each other, now becomes an annoying habit, because one of them didn't even let the other finish their own sentence. They dash back to the room, drawing an imaginary line in the bed, the bathroom, and all parts of the room, as they have now realized that the honeymoon, for all intents and purposes, is over.

But you should not be alarmed if conflict arises because conflict is a natural part of relationships. So, in addition to recognizing that your spouse is not going to complete you, you should also recognize that conflict is inevitable. The key here is how you handle it.

Studies have been conducted that provide predictors of successful marriages, but these can be skewed, as external factors impact a marriage throughout its tenure. It would be interesting to see an article that contrasts the costs that are spent by couples for rehearsal dinners, weddings and honeymoons, versus dollars spent meeting with pastors or other professionals for premarital counseling. No one can guarantee with 100% accuracy that any form of relationship counseling prior to marriage will ensure a "death do us part" marriage, but it is believed that it helps to reduce divorce figures by approximately 30%. I once heard an author of a book on relationships state that engagements and wedding planning can trigger a matrimania, which suggests a rush to be married, just for the sake of not being alone. This phenomenon seems to primarily affect women, as men seem not to be consumed by this mania.

Since men aren't given the same nudging toward commitment and/or marriage, it can lead to tension in the dating process, especially if their partner desires marriage and doesn't want dating to be a never-ending arrangement. Men have not been marketed to with the same vigor toward marriage; therefore, will be a more resistant customer when he finally decides on a purchase, he wants to ensure that buyer's remorse is minimized, and has second thoughts about returning the merchandise.

So when the honeymoon is over for a man, he resorts back to business as usual. He can return to his normal ritual of watching football games and participating in what may appear to his spouse to be a mundane life, but for him, it is what is comfortable. Men are very routine in nature, and don't like to have their habits disrupted because it can often result in a comical form of disorientation. For a man, it's not that he didn't enjoy the explorations and experiences of the honeymoon, but he is content to be back on his own soil, in his easy chair or in front of his favorite video game console.

When it comes to comparing this phase of a relationship, there is a technique that usually should be employed that can help one get through this precarious period. It's called a punt!

Sometimes You Have to Punt

If you are experiencing conflict in your marriage and you're locked in a battle with your spouse, sometimes it is better to let it go than to keep fighting. That's what the punt is all about on the gridiron (i.e., football field). A punt happens when the offense has advanced the ball as far as they can go without scoring. Essentially, they make a determination that it is more advantageous to give up the fight at that moment so that they gain a better field position on their next possession. Just as giving up the ball with a punt is beneficial when a team gets stuck on the gridiron, it can also be beneficial to give up an argument with your spouse. This can allow you time to cool down and regroup, and it can potentially save you from saying something that you might later regret.

Conflict often happens in the honeymoon phase of a relationship because, during the time in which the sweetest, most pleasurable part of your life together is supposed to occur, there can come some opposing factors that throw you off balance, making you question whether you have taken on the right partner for life. As you scramble to realize that the team is now falling apart, you no longer believe in a central goal, and you resort back to being the "star player" of your own team, fearing that your spouse might want to get out before they get stuck with some dead weight.

Although there is no central time span in which this honeymoon phase can occur, this "sweet" period can sometimes last from one month until the second year. There are some couples who are predestined to handle their adversities better than others, an idea that could lend itself to various theories of genetic make-up, as well as how a person has been raised to handle interpersonal challenges. On one hand, you can observe the couple who appears to be the most wholesome and to have all the right external features, such as physical touches and endearing words, but it could be these very couples who seem the most at risk, for their outward expressions merely mask their inability to handle conflicts, which are natural to any relationship.

When you reflect back on your college days, you probably had a first dormitory roommate who just seemed to rattle every nerve in your body, but somehow you survived your freshman year with him/her because each of you developed some effective coping skills, consisting of compromises, quiet retreats, and even some of the healthiest verbal arguments one could ever have. Sure, there were those who stormed out of their rooms, running down to the dorm adviser, stating that they weren't going to take this type of abuse anymore, and so the solution was to find another roommate or get a solitary dorm room. There are even situations where best friends go off to college with the anticipation that they are going to share everything, can't wait to experience sharing a room together, but soon experience a very interesting yet disturbing revelation.

While they had been in their separate spaces (their own homes) prior to going to college, they laughed, joked, and would even swap each other's clothes every now and then, but something happens to even these best of friends once they have to share a common space. It is discovered that each has different bedtimes and diverging musical tastes, and they even develop their own set of friends, as well as opposing cleaning styles. While the friends had once shared the same lunch, split the cost, or would each gladly pay for the other, now the familiarity of the relationship becomes more vague and there appears to be a sense of being taken for granted as their sharing begins to diminish to the point at which it comes to an abrupt end. Once they realize that their own personal glimpse of paradise is over, then everything that they seemed to enjoy about one another previously now annoys the other to no end.

This paradigm shift occurs in marriage. It is believed, and often encouraged, that one should always marry their best friend, someone who knows their ins and outs. Although they have this intimate knowledge of one's personal nuances, it would seem a natural fit that they would be the one to get along with you the best. Reflect back to the previous illustration about the dorm mates, and you will see some of the same dynamics occurring here because, although these characteristics were clearly known to one another prior to marriage, the intimacy of the details became even more magnified.

The once-open relationship now becomes one of over-analysis and accountability. That which was initially built on love and trust now becomes more based on personal sleuthing, as each must now give an account of every dollar spent and each movement in the day. The irony of this period in the relationship is that these have been trusted friends for quite some time, and now that the level of commitment expected has increased, so have the overall expectations that this couple now has for each other. We've all been there; the sniping, the shutting down, the angry words, the shouting matches, and even the quintessential nitpicking of finding fault in every little thing that is done or said. There appears to be a modal change in this newly birthed relationship, where a couple is married less than two years, and there are some emotions that begin to manifest now that most are neither familiar nor comfortable with. As a friend said, now begins the outpouring of the power plays, the depression, the outbursts of selfishness, and, most of all, the degrading words.

The Coin Toss

Remember the coin toss? Every football game begins with one. You recall that a coin toss is used to decide which team gets to receive the opening kickoff and thereby gets to go on offense first. The coin toss functions as an equalizer to ensure that each team has a 50/50 chance at an offensive possession and opportunity to score. Unfortunately, a 50/50 chance may be possible on the coin toss in football, but it doesn't work that way in a marriage.

One of the biggest fallacies usually shared with couples, especially prior to marriage, is that marriage is a 50/50 relationship; but if you consider the composite of a 50/50 ratio, you would find that anything that has these exact proportions is not capable of making any movement or changes. One is expected to give half and not a percentage more. This is like two bulls locking horns, trying to see which one can cross the tug-of-war line, but since each is exerting the same amount of force, never acquiescing to the other, the struggle will be endless, because it will always end in a draw, with no movement or formidable conclusion, nor a healthy solution. Marriages are based on changing ratios, and it is never clear, nor predictable, what form of ratio one will experience that day, that hour, or that minute. Since this is such an ever-changing variable, it adds to the spice of a relationship, for with it comes the removal of any form of predictability, always lending itself to some degree of spontaneity.

What is said next can be misconstrued, so that's the reason why this needs to be said in a very delicate manner, so as not to degrade, confuse, or be perceived as chauvinistic. In any arrangement, personal or social, there is at some point one party who will gain control to keep things moving along. This may be by a democratic process or by dictatorial persuasion, but whatever method is employed, someone has to take the lead. Corporations or small businesses that are established have partners that have certain degrees of controlling interests. A corporation typically appoints a board of directors whose responsibility it is to provide oversight of the corporation to make sure they adhere to the charter and goals established for said corporation. This is done for simple governance or out of necessity, to ensure that they protect from greed since, if a dominant partner tries to exercise his/her controlling interest, that can ruin the vibrancy of the organization. They are there to establish rules and a sense of fairness that will keep the corporation ethical and abiding by the rules.

All games come with a set of rules. The design of the rules is to ensure that those engaged in playing the game will participate in it fairly and adhere to them, so that all who desire to participate can enjoy the game. Whether it is Scrabble, Monopoly, rugby, or football, each of these games/sports has rules that help the players stay within the intended boundaries. In the absence of rules, there would be anarchy, which suggests that there is an absence of authority. To minimize this, in both games and sports, there are penalties that are implemented that punish the person who is responsible for an infraction, either through disobedience of the rules or through injury or violation of the other players.

Unnecessary Roughness and Other Penalties

In football, there are a few penalty calls that seem to parallel what often happens in relationships:

- Holding: Where an offensive player grabs part of the jersey of the defensive player.

- Clipping: A block below the waist from behind; usually causes injury to the other player.

- Malicious Unnecessary Roughness: Requires no definition.

- Unsportsmanlike conduct: Any verbal or physical abuse that diminishes the integrity of the sport.

Each one of these seems to address how to handle arguments or disagreements when unfair sparring takes place. One of the worst calls that can be made against a player is a "horse collar," also known as holding, where the player grabs the inside back of the opponent's shoulder pads, which is a vulnerable area that can cause serious injury. The result of such a grab could sling the player to the ground, often slamming their head onto the turf, which could result in a possible concussion. The goal of the offender is to bring the other person down by any means they can.

Whether it's pulling the opponent's facemask or the horse collar, both are considered to be unsportsmanlike in nature, and just like in a relationship, they are considered to be penalties that will result in the loss of yards for the one committing the penalty, causing the team to be farther away from their intended goal.

Clipping is just as bad, as most of us are familiar with the saying "hit him or her below the belt." This area of the body is most vulnerable, as the genitalia are the life producers in the human body. Any massive injury to this area can decrease the possibility of life ever coming forth from this reproductive area. In professional sports, this danger is most times minimized because great care is taken to ensure that a cup or other protective gear is used to guard this sensitive area. But when left unguarded, and when the intent of the other party is to take a shot where one might be the most vulnerable, this is also referred to as a cheap shot. Think of the many cheap shots that you've personally taken at someone. Most of the time, this is in the form of derogatory comments or mental abuse, with the full intent of damaging the psyche of the other person.

There was a chant that we recited in my childhood, which is commonly heard and spoken even today. It says, "Sticks and stones may break my bones, but words will never hurt me." What a giant fallacy! If we sustained broken bones at some point in our lifetime, there may be little evidence of that injury's effect many years later, but reflect on negative comments you heard from a parent, teacher, friend, or co-worker that still haunt your mind today. It makes you shudder to realize the power, sting, and long-lasting effects words that are used to willfully attack another can have, borne out of the disdain for oneself and reflecting a poor self-image.

Unnecessary roughness and unsportsmanlike conduct really require no explanation. In the very structure of both words, the prefix is "un," which means "not." There is roughness in a relationship that is not necessary and there is conduct that is clearly not sportsmanlike. These two take away from what should be a fair and equitable partnership but that instead focuses on destruction rather than edification.

It takes years to erect a soaring skyscraper, but as we unfortunately saw in the tragedy of September 11, 2001, it takes seconds to destroy one. Confidence in oneself can be many years in the making, but can be damaged in the blink of an eye by injurious words and actions. So you must be thoughtful in your relationship, even when the honeymoon is over. It is what you say, as well as how you say it, that matters.

Let's take a look at some of the calls that are made by the referee during the game that are synonymous to football, as well as relationships. These are the calls, if repeated too often for the remainder of the game, could cause the team to lose valuable yardage, and potential points.

Unsportsmanlike Conduct

There are certain things that you just shouldn't do in football. Fighting and other unsportsmanlike conduct are among them. In football, unsportsmanlike conduct is an offense that violates the rules of the game. Not only will the player face a penalty, but the entire team can suffer and face sanctions. When players engage in unsportsmanlike conduct, the team suffers a 15-yard penalty and the player may be ejected from the game. Players should avoid unsportsmanlike conduct at all costs, since the loss of 15 yards can result in the loss of momentum and could even jeopardize the game.

Fighting in marriage? Is this something that really exists, or is this simply a mythical perception of how couples get their issues settled? We are not necessarily talking about the physical type of fighting, which often and unfortunately does occur, but for our purposes here, we will be talking about the verbal form. My spouse and I have discussed this fighting phenomenon on numerous occasions, and as a woman, I still disagree with his version, but definitely understand his perspective. He has told me several times that a man's goal when he gets involved in a fight is to win. He will usually do anything to ensure his win, and in my opinion, he will cheat, play dirty, or use any other tactic to make sure that he comes out victorious. But much like in football, unsportsmanlike conduct in a marriage should be avoided at all costs.

Although our society has changed in its recognition and appreciation of women involved in athletic and combat-type sports, it is a very rare breed of women that engages in cage fighting, professional and amateur wrestling, professional boxing, or other contact sports. These are games and sports in which men are able to release some form of pent-up testicular energy, but where their primary purpose is to beat the crap out of their opponents. You don't hear of women involved in beer brawls; however, as you know, there are rare instances of them physically fighting over a man. You don't hear of them racing down the street in side-by-side duels with muscle cars, and you definitely don't hear of them shooting people just to resolve arguments (self-defense, yes, revenge, no). So what is it about men and their need to win? When it comes to matters of verbal discourse or just having an in-depth conversation, one might ask, since men are supposedly the logical gender, why it seems that they become so discombobulated when they are pressed to the mat in what we deem as a difference of opinion.

Man, as part of the primary species from his primeval days, was used to going out to hunt for his food, and since he had to fend for his family, his responsibility was to bring home the bacon, and no excuses were accepted. Therefore, whatever traps he had to set for animals or vermin, he would become very creative, as his goal was to win. He knew that he had to be victorious, and anything less than that would be unacceptable. This might seem like a comical illustration, but if you really ponder it, you would see the reality of what I'm saying, because men are just not used to losing at *anything!* This is not a comfortable place for him, for confrontation is not his best suit of amour. His desire is still to win. So goes the colloquial phrase "winning isn't everything," which is always uttered by the loser. Losing! Who really wants to be the loser, and is there really such a thing as a gracious loser? Women don't like to lose either. We are aggressive and have become even more vocal in our aggression. Especially when it comes to our own gender, we surely don't want to be a loser either. Think of the rite that takes place prior to every spring known as the Bridal Dress Sale, or the one that takes place every Christmas holiday that's called the Black Friday Specials. Open up the doors, and the women, whose only goal is to the obtain the dress or sales item of their choice, flood in. At that point, every other woman is the enemy, and she must be silenced, shoved, and shaken, until the very death grip she has on that coveted item is released, so that it might fall into the hands of a more worthy recipient—me! You think this is too drastic of an example? Consider the soccer mom who wants Timmy to play on the soccer team but has been told that he has been cut from trials to accommodate a more worthy player. Uh-oh, oh no you didn't! Step back and watch the sparks fly, as "Soccer Mom" is not about to take no for an answer, especially when she just got through helping the kids with homework, got her shins bruised by helping Timmy practice, and last but not least, has already purchased the necessary uniform and equipment, as she knew beyond a shadow of a doubt that her little "Pelé" would assuredly be chosen over less talented competitors.

MARRIAGE PLAYBOOK
COACHING STRATEGY
Second Quarter: The Honeymoon Is Over

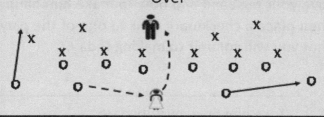

- Know that all butterflies have a season. Once the flutter of love leaves your stomach, that doesn't mean that you've fallen out of love. Love is not just a feeling, but you must love them until they feel it.

- Kiss each other (on the lips) as you leave each morning and as you return home each night.

- Take five minutes to listen to how their day went without interruption or judgment.

- If you have children, make sure that you establish a good relationship with a sitter or relatives who can watch your child, so that you can go out at least once every two weeks.

- Don't forget to laugh with and at each other.

Your Love Touchdown Playlist

Take a look at these plays to find out how to love your husband and how to make him happy; then place a checkmark next to one of the plays that you will commit to making today.

- Take him on a mystery date.
- Blow him a kiss.
- Send him a flirty text.
- Ask for his opinion about something.
- Give him a backrub.
- Make a list of the great things he's done.
- Sleep in the nude when you're angry.

What are some of the key points that you have learned from this section?

_____

_____

_____

What type of playbook strategy would you develop to improve or keep your relationship consistent?

_____

_____

_____

If you were providing advice to a friend based on what you read in this section, what would be the one key takeaway?

_____

_____

_____

HALFTIME
Reviewing the First Half

The score is 28 to 10 and it is halftime; but who's been keeping score? You are, of course. So far, it's consisted of a couple of touchdowns, along with kicks for the extra point, and the other team hasn't fared as well. They have played a good, aggressive game, but have only managed to get one touchdown and a field goal. During the game, there has been a lot of movement on the field, but there have also been a number of penalty flags thrown along the way. Both teams feel as though they have played a good game, and believe they've gotten some unfair calls as well. Where some of these plays are considered to be a part of the game, others command stiff penalties and most times warrant being put on the bench, hoping that the player who caused the infraction would realize the serious consequences of their actions.

This is the part of the game where the teams retire to their respective locker rooms for refreshment, rest and hopefully a pep talk, to review the pluses and minuses that have been achieved in the first two quarters. This period of respite only lasts 12 minutes. If you're on the winning side, it's probably the best 12 minutes, but if you're losing, it is probably a very painful 12 minutes.

The score is pretty evident, as it's easy to see on the jumbo Tron, who has had the advantage. Even at this juncture, it is still anyone's game, because there are two more quarters of playing time, and this is definitely not the time to give up. This is the time to review the plays that were called, watch the film to see if there were some actions that took place on the field that could definitely have been avoided, and how do they strategize to get their edge back.

As we have pointed out, in both genders, neither likes to lose; therefore, is compromise an easy thing to accomplish or consider? After the first two quarters of a football game, there is time to retire to the locker room and do a quick review of some of the perfect and flawed plays, with the goal of trying to ensure that the next half assures a win. This is the time in which the coach has a chance to reprimand the stupid mistakes, as well as to reward those who contributed to putting points on the board. Those who might have been wounded along the way, who got some bandages on the sideline, are now able to have more attention given to the issues at hand. An astute coach points out that they could have avoided some unnecessary flags. Flags are not celebratory items that are thrown in the air, but are visual indicators that someone has noticed that a play, move, or action resulted in a transgression of the rules of the playbook. Each player knows the playbook and the rules of the game, but when engaged in heavy combat, the focus on what's right is lost, and focus is instead placed on winning and being successful by any means necessary.

So as the coach looks at the clock and notices that the time that he has had to rally the troops during this period of rest is just about over, there is a shift in one's mindset to concentrate and get the adrenaline flowing. There are just a few minutes left to acknowledge the team's mistakes in the first half, regroup if there have been feelings hurt, and get back out to the field, for there is not much time to rest before the alarm sounds to start the second half. In a relationship, when both parties have sparred for a while and feel that they are tired and disgusted, this temporary retreat can be refreshing, but it can also be menacing and diabolical, as the respective couples decide whether they want to play a fair game or really push the envelope and go for the win.

How to Play Fair

As we have already stated, conflict is inevitable in a marriage, but it is important not to cross certain boundaries. The key to fighting is to fight fair, which means being civil toward each other and making it more of a discussion than an argument. Whether you're having a disagreement about money, physical intimacy, or extended family, be sure to be respectful and listen to the other person's opinions. Use the following tips to help your arguments and disagreements become productive.

- **Identify the issues.** Sometimes couples have recurring disagreements that always seem to surface. Generally, there is an underlying theme for every recurring disagreement and the problem cannot be solved until these themes are identified. If you want to have more productive disagreements, be sure to put in the work to understand what the real issues are.

- **Start with agreement.** You can realize a vast improvement in your arguments by presenting the issues in a softer way. This means never starting with criticism. It may take a little practice, but there is always something you can agree on. Starting your discussions with agreement is the best way to ensure that everyone plays fair and disagreements don't turn into arguments.

- **Listen more and talk less.** When you're in the heat of an argument, there's always the tendency to talk fast to get your point out. But if you take a breath and pause before you open your mouth, this can be an effective way to approach the conversation in a calmer manner. Not only will this lessen your chances of saying something that you will regret later, but it will show the other person that you care about their opinions too.

- **Say "I" instead of "you."** Nothing can derail a conversation more quickly than accusing your spouse of screwing up. That's what they hear when you continually use the word "you," as in "you did something wrong." Instead, try to communicate how you feel, as in, "I felt bad when you said that." Using the word "I" helps your spouse understand the impact of what they did and avoids placing the blame on them.

- **Avoid character assaults.** Your arguments should never devolve into personal attacks. Instead of name-calling, be sure to focus on the issues. Calling your spouse offensive names is definitely not playing fair. It's degrading, and your words can have a lasting impact on your relationship. For example, if your spouse doesn't do the dishes or mow the lawn, don't call them shiftless or lazy; instead, just tell them how it makes you feel that those chores are not done.

- **Don't threaten to leave.** One of the worst things you can do during an argument is to threaten to leave. Sometimes emotions can flare up during a heated argument, but it is never a good idea to make those types of threats. If you are working toward a healthy relationship, divorce should never be an option.

- **Never resort to abuse.** Neither party should ever resort to physical, emotional, or psychological abuse. Fighting with your spouse is healthy only as long as it remains fair and safe. You should seek outside intervention if any sort of abuse ever occurs.

- **Repeat what you heard.** Repeat back what you have heard and not what you think the person said. Repeating the other person's idea is a great way to show that you were listening and that you understand what was being said.

- **Don't dominate the conversation.** Give each other ample, equal time when responding. Dominating the conversation can make things go awry because it may be seen as insensitive and controlling.

- **Avoid saying "You Never."** Don't start a sentence with "You Always" or "You Never". This is an indication that you are hurting or that your needs are not being met. These types of statements are generally used to emphasize your position but are not taken seriously because they seldom true. They are also accusatory in a self-pitying kind of way.

It is important to recognize that all couples fight sometimes. That is a natural part of being in a relationship with another individual. So there is no need to assume that your marriage is doomed simply because you had an argument. But just like halftime is a good time to review in football, it is also a good time to review your marriage. Halftime in marriage can be a healthy respite to allow you and your mate to discuss strategies on how you are going to move forward in order to continue effectively loving each other. As a couple, establish "Couples Goals" and plan how to implement them together.

Remember these 6 R's:

Retreat. You and your spouse retreat to a special place, away from all distractions and the noise of life to concentrate on each other for the improvement of your life together.

Refreshments. Teams build their strength back up by hydrating with water, Gatorade, and energy bars. Clear your minds by reminiscing with each other about those fulfilling attributes that once attracted you to each other.

Recovery. This is when additional stretching of certain body parts is attended to before the start of the next half. Find a marriage mentor or Christian marriage counselor to assist with one or more areas of your marriage that might be causing pain, angst, hurt, or emotional distress.

Recap. Recap the gains, losses, strengths, and weakness of your team. Ensure that you are focusing on the gains and how to strengthen the weak areas.

Re-strategize. Decide what is necessary to score with your spouse that makes them feel loved and respected. Create a strategy that is not fault-finding, but rather one of mutual acceptance.

Reenergize. All teams periodically need motivation, and sometimes develop their own fight song to inspire them to victory. Find workshops, retreats, and classes that can challenge and motivate you as a couple to move in the same direction.

The 6 R's are a great way to strategize and set goals for your marriage. And now that you've had a chance to strategize your relationship, spend a few moments taking our Halftime Quiz to review the pluses and minuses in your marriage.

2 minute wrap-up

What are some of the key points that you have learned from this section?

_____

_____

_____

What type of playbook strategy would you develop to improve or keep your relationship consistent?

_____

_____

_____

If you were providing advice to a friend based on what you read in this section, what would be the one key takeaway?

_____

_____

HALFTIME
RELATIONSHIP QUIZ

Directions: Read each football play and then take a look at how it applies to relationships. Respond to each question by circling YES or NO as appropriate. When you're done, add up all of your points.

Hail Mary: A long pass that barely has a "wing and a prayer" of being caught by a team player. A Hail Mary is basically a last ditch effort to salvage a bad situation.

Relationship Application: Have you ever had a situation where you made a last ditch effort to salvage your relationship because you tried everything you could think of but nothing else seemed to work?

YES = 0   NO = 7

Fake Field Goal: A situation where one team appears as though they are going to kick the ball, but instead, they fake the kick and another player either throws or runs with the ball. In essence, a Fake Field Goal is a trick play where the team gives the illusion of doing one thing, but pulls a switch and does something different.

Relationship Application: Have you ever had a situation where you and your spouse have agreed to achieve a common goal, and at the last minute, one of you decides to do something completely opposite without informing the other?

YES = 0   NO = 7

Fake Punt: The Fake Punt is a trick play similar to the Fake Field Goal where it appears that the team is going to kick the ball, but at the last minute, they do something different.

Relationship Application: Have you ever promised to do something that is meaningful for the relationship but backed out at the last minute because you were upset by something he did?

YES = 0   NO = 7

End Around: Another trick play where a wide receiver goes around the back to hand the ball directly to the quarterback.

Relationship Application: Has one of you ever gone behind the other's back in order to get your way or achieve your goal?

YES = 0   NO = 7

Play Action Pass: A surprise play that is intended to look as though a team will run the ball, but they shrewdly turn it into a pass instead, potentially gaining more yards than expected.

Relationship Application: Have your spouse ever expected you to treat them one way, but you completely surprise them by considering their needs, and favored them in a much more pleasant manner?

YES = 7   NO = 0

Taking a Safety: A Safety occurs when the offense downs the ball in their own end zone opposed to being tackled. They safely sacrifice 2 points instead of giving the other team a chance for a 6 point turnover.

Relationship Application: Have you ever known that you were right and your spouse was wrong, but you played it safe and gave in to keep the peace?

YES = 7   NO = 0

Squib Kick: When a ball is intentionally kicked low, making it harder for the receiving team to get because it keeps bouncing around uncontrollably.

Relationship Application: Have you ever purposely avoided dealing with your spouse on a sensitive subject because you couldn't accept their solution even though you know they were right?

YES = 0   NO = 7

Victory Formation: A Victory Formation occurs when the offense has the lead in the game, especially as the time clock is running out, and they want to ensure a win. The quarterback typically kneels while having possession of the ball, while the rest of the team lines up in a winning formation.

Relationship Application: Have you ever verbally praised your spouse around others for being the person that you know you were blessed with?

YES = 7   NO = 0

How Did Your Relationship Score?

Score of 0-14: Your relationship could use some improvement. You and your spouse should have serious and loving dialogue about the things that matter to you.

Score of 21-35: Your relationship is on the right track but could use a little work. Take some time to honestly review each play so that you can evaluate what is working and what is not.

Score of 42-56: Your relationship is in great shape! Keep up the good work and don't forget to keep getting better.

THIRD QUARTER

Reworking the Offense and Defense

After completing the restful period known as halftime, the players get to do something that they didn't get to do in the first two quarters. The players will all maintain their same playing positions, but for the remaining quarters, they switch sides, allowing them to gain a different perspective on the field by going in the opposite direction than they had been playing. In a relationship, this could be paralleled to being given the opportunity to see the other spouse's point of view, similar to what we know as walking in someone else's shoes. For a long time it has been said that you never know how a person really feels until you've had a chance to walk in their moccasins or high heels. If the first half of the game resulted in the one team playing with the glare of the sun in their eyes, this may have given the other team an unfair advantage, handicapping them or just making it more difficult for them to perform. Now that the second team gets to experience the same set of conditions, it can be determined if the first team was really a well-oiled machine or if they were just operating with an advantage for the first half of the game.

It is also during this quarter that, if prior to halftime the scores for each team were remarkably close, there comes a rush of adrenaline, as the teams pour onto the field again, realizing that they have got to play harder and smarter in order to get a touchdown. Since the prior quarters had seen so many flags, interceptions made, and turnovers sacrificed, it is now time that the referees and coaches pay close attention to the true adherence to game rules, ensuring that the game is played fairly and that the guidelines are followed to help minimize injury to those involved.

The Offensive Line

Now that we're in the third quarter, the entire team, including the offensive line, is expected to execute certain adjustments that were made during halftime. The offensive line is a group of offensive players that assemble across the line of scrimmage, which is simply the spot on the field from which the football is hiked. One of the primary jobs of the offensive line is to protect the quarterback. Frequently, the offensive line will encircle the quarterback to create a barrier that is known as a pocket. In your marriage, this pocket represents a wall of protection that is symbolic of the boundaries needed to protect your relationship from intrusions.

There are countless things that can encroach on your marriage, but we believe that there are three general categories of intrusions that your marriage must be protected against: emotions, interactions, and time.

Emotions play a crucial role in your relationships. Whether it is affection, validation, sympathy, or security, it is important to guard yourself against giving away the emotions that belong to your spouse. Even venting to a friend of the opposite sex can sometimes be problematic since sharing your heart with someone else could create a bond with that person. You should also be cautious about sharing your feelings and dreams with someone of the opposite sex because it could bring about an emotional connection that could turn an innocent rendezvous into a passionate affair.

The **interactions** you have with the world around you can also cause undesirable encroachments into your marriage. Therefore, it is very important to be cautious about who you choose to interact with. The need to be guarded with your words and text messages is probably obvious, but you should be aware that even your body language can send messages to someone of the opposite sex. The same is true of having lunch or dinner engagements, or just hanging out too much with friends who your spouse doesn't know.

Time is a critical element of your relationship, but it is one of those things that can get away from you without you even noticing. Because of the incredibly fast pace of the world we live in, it is almost impossible to disconnect and devote some quality time to your spouse. Sometimes you and your spouse can be in the same room, and one of you is distracted by Facebook while the other is intently watching reality TV. In order to spend some quality time together, you might try scheduled date nights, cooking dinner together, playing a board game, or binge-watching your favorite television show.

In football, offense means engaging the opponent or taking action against the other team with the objective of scoring points. In your marriage, offense means taking the initiative to protect your relationship from intrusions on the outside. Offense is an ongoing responsibility in your marriage, but it's worth the effort.

The Defensive Coordinator

On the other side of the offense is the defense. This is the quarter in which the experiences of both the offensive and defensive coordinator are key. They have watched the game carefully, noticing the weaknesses of their own players and the strength of the opposition.

A defensive coordinator is a coach responsible for the team's defense. These coordinators are a coveted breed of individuals, as they have shown their skills while coaching other teams, whether on the collegiate or professional level. Their expertise is just as critical as that of those who are executing the plays on the field, for it is their responsibility to stand on the sidelines and watch the various plays that have been called. They have observed the blitzes, the Statue of Liberty plays, and any other noticeable play that should call attention to the need to win, as there is only one quarter following this one. These coordinators are sought out from across the country, but the main reason they are chosen is because they have a track record of success.

The defensive coordinator tries to ensure that the ball will not move forward, and the offensive coordinator tries to ensure that it will. This leads to some interesting dynamics, as the goal of any game is to come away with a win. Each side desires to win and never to settle for a loss. Therefore, it should be emphasized that the key is winning. Yes, how the game is played is just as important, but the ultimate goal is to win. This can be accomplished through field goals, forcing turnovers, kicking for the extra point, interceptions, and anything else that will give one the most points for a victory.

This third-quarter concept can be applied in a marital relationship, irrespective of the ages of the people involved or how long they have been married. When mental and physical fatigue begin to invade a relationship, it can feel as though things are now at the eleventh hour and there does not appear to be any relief in sight. The goal line is within reach, but trying to make a first down seems to be more elusive than ever, and all you want to do is to succeed.

Many marriages have reached this point, as they have experienced some unnecessary roughness along the way, or just slipped into a quiet state of complacency. Whether it's been five years or 50 years, there are situations along the way that can paralyze or handicap the relationship, and it tends to limp along for what may seem to be an eternity. There is a mythical rule that states that if you have made it past the first seven years of your marriage, then you are pretty much home free. I'm not quite sure what home they are referring to or what constitutes this freedom. This old tale dates back to movies of the '50s that always saw the number seven as a lucky number, while at the same time, it was also to be regarded as the time in which there was some unreachable "itch" that couldn't be scratched. By the seven-year-mark, a couple has learned how to adjust to each other's idiosyncrasies and not be uprooted by tantrums or mood swings, and how to simply move on with the rest of their days.

Impedegate: Cheating on the Sideline

Cheating happens! It happens in football and it happens in marriage. Take the game in 2013 between the Pittsburgh Steelers and the Baltimore Ravens. It was dubbed "Impedegate" because the Steelers coach tried to impede a 73-yard touchdown by tripping a Baltimore Ravens wide receiver. Clearly this was cheating, and the coach was flagged for unsportsmanlike conduct, but the damage was done.

The reason cheating happens in football is obvious: to win. But why would a husband cheat in a perfectly good marriage?

When an itch of infidelity that has been scratched has crept in, it can create a great degree of anxiety for any couple, especially for the member of the couple who was not responsible for the indiscretion. In no way is infidelity or the acceptance of it condoned, but a strong marriage can often use this painful experience as a gauge of where they should have been addressing each other's needs. If the partners deal with the infidelity with maturity and weigh the benefits of the relationship, this does not have to result in the termination of what has been, to this point, a trusting, loving partnership. Here are five reasons a husband may cheat on a faithful and devoted spouse:

- **Immaturity.** Maturity comes with experience, not with age, so if your husband does not have a lot of experience in committed relationships, he may not be mature enough to understand the implications of his sexual misadventure. Immature men tend to be inconsiderate and only think about themselves. That means that they act based on impulse rather than thoughtful decisions.

- **Addiction.** Whether it be drugs, sex, or alcohol, addiction is another factor that can cause infidelity. If your spouse has already been discovered to have had an outside relationship, an addiction could make it spiral out of control since it can lower inhibitions and can reduce the judgment of the addict. There may be times when a spouse considered cheating and didn't do it, but made the decision after becoming high or intoxicated, or used substances as an excuse to follow through.

- **Anger.** Anger is a strong feeling of displeasure or hostility and can be a significant motivator of infidelity. If a husband feels hurt in his relationship, either intentionally or unintentionally, it could cause him to want to get even with his spouse. This is especially true if the couple has an unhealthy pattern of fighting. If you are in a marriage where some deep-seated anger issues exist, your best bet is to seek help immediately.

- **Insecurity.** A person is more likely to cheat on their spouse if they are insecure in the relationship. They may have a personal complex and feel that they are not good enough or that they are not truly lovable. Whatever the case may be, if your spouse has some displeasure with themselves, it may be time to seek help.

- **Unhappiness.** It would be a mistake to think that every man who cheats does so because he is unhappy. That being said, research has shown that nearly half of all men who cheat do so because their physical or emotional needs are not being met. This simply means that they are unhappy with their current relationship. Men have a great need to feel valued and supported. If a man is unhappy, he may be feeling underappreciated, or he might just need a shoulder to cry on. His personal unhappiness should not be a crutch for his actions, as one person should never be charged with keeping someone else happy. Get in control of your own emotions.

Cheating is never a good thing, but once you have an idea of the triggers to infidelity, you will be in a better position to be on guard. No matter what the reason, cheating is a very hurtful and emotional experience; however, it doesn't have to mean the end of the relationship. If both spouses want to be together and are committed to making the relationship work, there is a good chance that you can get through it. Be prepared to know that there will be those who are critical of your decision to work it out, but they should be mindful of their own motives, especially if their intervention or advice is not in the best interest of the couple.

Some couples feel as though they are in the third quarter of their relationship, but most don't feel as though the combined effort is a win, but rather that each side has developed a keen defensive strategy, making sure that the other one does not move forward or get a perceived advantage. In the game of chess, this might be called a stalemate, for this is when the result is a deadlock, because there does not seem to be any plan that will allow them to move ahead and win. This is the stage when complacency seems to set in, and it is not only present in unhealthy marriages. Most times it is not noticed by the participants themselves, but by those who are standing on the sidelines, noticing that the couple's normal stride is getting a little slower and that which was once roaring, passionate fire has now simmered into embers.

If the union has brought forth children, they can often become the focal point of the relationship, with the spouses paying more attention to their children than to their mate. This is not to insinuate that parenting should ever be set on the back burner, but often, children are moved to the front burners while the relationship is allowed to be set on low or simmer, falling into neglect. Children require and demand a lot of attention. The infancy stage is a 24-hour responsibility and involves diaper changes, a nursing/bottle regimen, and countless nights of walking the floor to rock a colicky baby to sleep. We've known couples who have used their tiny infant as a bed divider, giving them a reason not to have any sense of connection or intimacy. They have allowed themselves to reach this point of separation and don't even recognize their actions until someone else brings it to their attention. A cocoon begins to build around their emotions, and the callus of the cocoon shell becomes even tougher without them even noticing. All they see is that they are going through the routine of normal days, and to them, nothing really appears to be different. This morphs into a mundane existence and is usually the stage in one's life when they begin to ask themselves if they are happy with the way that their individual life has been trending and the fact that all of their sacrifices have been for others, with very little emphasis on their own mental and physical health. This is when each day blends into night, creating an endless cycle without them noticing that their spouse has been orbiting in their own world, since the children have become the core of their universe while they have shelved their own unmet needs. They are now forced to relinquish their own desire for attention.

This sense of loss can also occur in couples who have no children. It is easy to incorrectly assume that these couples have the most productive marriages because they lack the responsibility of having the little tikes pulling on their coattails every day, but theirs is a different form of separation. Couples that have children may consider their children to be a common goal and sometimes shamefully use them as emotional scapegoats for the next 18 years. The childless couple can put a lot of focus on climbing the rungs of their own career ladders, not realizing that they have been focusing solely on their own ambitions and goals. This is acceptable when a person has chosen to cohabitate with someone, but when the relationship calls for a lifelong partnership, it takes the commitment to an entirely different level.

Any pause in the current football season caused by threats of lockouts or negotiation breakdowns, the sport could lose a great deal of its monetary value. When these delays occur, it often results in a player's loss of continuity, as they lose the ability to build a cohesive relationship during a shortened season. This reduces their opportunity to learn each other's personalities, as well as leading to them missing out on the important skill of knowing how to read the other players' strengths and weaknesses. Why is this so important to discuss during the third quarter? It is in this quarter when they've rested from halftime and need to quickly re-energize and turn on the cylinders to get the engine running again. The two-minute warning will sound in the fourth quarter, and the squeeze of these tense moments will solely depend upon how well teammates know that they can read and depend on each other.

This is where we get to appreciate the value of a well-paid and experienced coach. According to Forbes.com, Bill Belichick, head coach of the New England Patriots, is probably one of the highest-paid coaches in the NFL, topping out in 2019 with an annual salary of $12.5 million dollars. There are many other coaches in the NFL that don't trail too far behind him, which would lead one to ask, Why they are paid so much?

When a manager is paid to oversee their team, they shoulder a huge responsibility, and they must have the emotional intelligence to be able to deal with the myriad of personalities, rants, and temperaments of those who make up their team. They must be adept to know the moods and the skills of each player, and they must know when to put each player in the game or when to pull them out. They have to know when to let them catch their breath and when their expertise will benefit the field at the most critical point in the game, regardless of how tired the player might be.

If you have ever participated in a sport, then you are keenly aware that one can "hit the wall" of fatigue and be ready to call it quits, even though the game is far from being over. I've sat there and watched coaches call a player off the field, whisper something into their ear, and slap them on the butt, and then the player charges back on the field as though nothing ever happened.

There comes a moment when the role of the coach must be most respected, when they become both confronter and inspirer. Team members are often fueled by an excess of adrenalin, that they begin to react by instinct rather than focusing strategically on trying to win the game. This is when you see the most egregious penalties are made because there is anger, disappointment, and definitely fear that they could lose, especially when they had a winning edge. This is when clear-headed, unbiased leadership is imperative, to get the hotheads in line, out of their feelings, and attentive to the task.

So what's the correlation with marriage? In a relationship, it should not matter who you or your spouse talks with to gain wise counsel, as long as that person is pointing your spouse back to you, and, if they have erred in their ways, in the right direction. Don't become so stuck on yourself in pride that you say that, "If I'm his or her best friend, then I expect him or her to talk with *me* about everything." In the heat of a situation, and if your mate is the source of your discontent, it will not be an effective strategy to believe that only the two of you can solve the immediate problem. Too often we've heard this statement from individuals, but it is a cry for help, expressing that all they want to do is be heard and respected. It's better that you never lose sight of the fact that there are others who have more experience than you do in certain areas, and who will do all they can to assist you, but not enable you.

There are many coaches in various sporting outlets who have not only coached their current teams, but have coached other teams and players, and have a broader perspective on how to handle more situations than you do.

Can You Still Win the Game?

We've already stated the difficult challenge that is undertaken when infidelity invades the sacred space of marriage. One of the biggest hurdles to repairing your relationship is rebuilding the trust. How do you know that the cheating is over? How can you ever trust your cheating spouse again? Is it worth remaining in a relationship with this person? These are valid questions that you must answer.

A marriage counselor may be able to help you get through the ordeal, but, if you pay attention, you may be able to see some signs that your marriage is salvageable. One of the first signs is that your partner has broken off all contact with the other person. They should inform you of any attempts by the other person to contact him as well. You should also looks for signs that your partner is doing everything he can to restore your trust in them. And one of the most important signs that you may be able to salvage the marriage is that your partner exhibits a lot of patience and is open and honest in answering all of your questions. As my wife often asks women who confide in her, "Do you *really* want to know the whole truth, and if so, are you prepared to handle it?" Just as with the relationships we have with our children, we have to give them a "safe" space, void of judgment, to receive and accept the truth. If you decide to work on the marriage, be sure that you and your spouse are on the same page. If he is serious about working on the relationship, here are some things he should do, as well as some things you should do.

Things He Should Do

- They must be willing to admit that what they did was wrong without placing blame.
- They must be willing to do everything they can to earn your trust again. Accountability is key.
- They must be willing to never cross that line again. Boundaries must be set.
- They must be willing to listen to you express your disappointment over and over.
- They must be willing to get professional help.
- They must be willing to understand what your needs are in the relationship.

Things You Should Do

- You must be open and honest with them about your emotions, anger, fears, and disappointment.
- You must seek to understand why they cheated.
- You must consider participating in marriage counseling.
- You must take the time to care for yourself.

If a spouse has cheated (this is not gender-specific), it is important to acknowledge that it will take time to heal. This can be synonymous with going through the stages of grief.

Just remember that offense means taking the initiative to protect your relationship from intrusions on the outside. Defense means doing those things to prevent cheating in the first place. Of course, no one can ever guarantee that their spouse won't be unfaithful, but if they do, don't be afraid to get outside counsel to help repair your relationship. In the long run, you may find that it is worth it.

MARRIAGE PLAYBOOK
COACHING STRATEGY
Third Quarter: Reworking the Offense and Defense

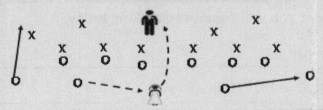

- At the first sign of trouble, seek out help. It's easier to give first aid when love has been injured than when the pain of it is hemorrhaging.

- Model the behavior you would want your children to display when they marry.

- Find a few mentoring couples who will be honest with you and will not allow you to use your spouse as a scapegoat.

- Guard your relationship from infidelity. An investment needs to be protected and requires regular loving deposits to ensure proper growth. Don't hold back your love and sex in order to punish your spouse.

- Read books, attend seminars, and go on weekend retreats to hone the skill of preserving your relationship.

Your Love Touchdown Playlist

Take a look at these plays to find out how to love your husband and how to make him happy; then place a checkmark next to one of the plays that you will commit to making today.

- Pray for him.
- Buy tickets to the big game.
- Make him breakfast in bed.
- Take the garbage out for him.
- Give him a free night out with his guys.
- Take a shower together.
- Play a board game together.

What are some of the key points that you have learned from this section?

_____

_____

_____

What type of playbook strategy would you develop to improve or keep your relationship consistent?

_____

_____

_____

If you were providing advice to a friend based on what you read in this section, what would be the one key takeaway?

_____

_____

FOURTH QUARTER
Winning the Game

The fourth quarter opens, and it's been a tight game. Oddly enough, both are home teams, but their scores are completely different because one side has analyzed the other side more intensely and has a greater desire to win. As a result of some well-executed plays in the third quarter, Home Team 1 (wife) seems to have a clear advantage over Home Team 2 (husband), as she has kept her body full of emotional Gatorade to compensate for the exhaustion that she has endured during the last quarter. There were some close calls, as well as some fouls that were clearly seen by the referee, as they were both too engaged in the game to notice that they had gone offside or out of bounds, trying to get to the goal line.

Team attitude is critical at this juncture. The quarterback, who handles the execution of the called plays, is just about exhausted after three long quarters, and he may become weary at this point, knowing that his throwing arm has reached its peak. This could result in sloppy execution of plays, sacks, fumbles, or other things that now make him more vulnerable than ever. Because the game has been fought heroically, it's getting close to the end, and victory is just about 15 minutes away.

This is when the rubber really meets the road. Tires get their greatest amount of wear and tear when there is little tread left on them. Whenever I've taken my car to have someone check out the tires, rather than replacing the tires, my mechanic asks me the question, "Have you ever rotated or balanced your tires before?" The first time this was asked of me, I know that I must have tilted my head, squinted one eye, and then let the words roll from my lips, "What are you talking about?" This is when the service person, if they are operating in an ethical manner, will not try to sell me a new set of tires, but will let me know that to get the maximum use out of my tires, I need to change things around in order to give proper balance to the vehicle. Since each tire has two equal sides of tread, there are at least eight different tire arrangements that can be made on my car to give the tires longer life.

Every relationship gets to a point of stagnation where it may seem old, dull, and lifeless. Just like tires, relationships hit a lot of potholes, and the natural proclivity is to immediately change the tires or replace the entire vehicle for a newer model.

Reflecting on the early days of playground equipment, there was an apparatus that kids played on called a seesaw. Even at an early age, we were exposed to and participated in the aspects of physics without even realizing it. A piece of board was strategically placed over a midpoint, and two people, hopefully not of widely varying weight distribution, would sit on opposite sides of the midpoint. They would bounce up and down, each hoisting the other one up in the air, but if they wanted to frustrate the other person so they couldn't go much higher, they would shift their weight on one side to ensure that they would produce an unbalanced effect. Later in life, we would learn from a physics teacher that this fulcrum point was necessary for us to engage in the child's play that gave us so much joy. If the board is not properly aligned at the desired fulcrum point, regardless of the effort put forth, peak performance would be thwarted. So what's the takeaway? Balance. It is essential to the lifespan of a healthy relationship. Anything out of balance has negative consequences, whether it's a checking account, a seesaw, or life itself.

Too many fights and not enough compliments in a relationship will knock it off of its fulcrum. It boils down to strategy and tenacity. When a team knows that it's losing but still desires to win, it has to dig down deep to get the willpower to hang in there when it seems as though all the odds are against it. It is about having the mindset that you and your teammates can win this game.

We've seen football games where you could have predicted who the winner was going to be because there wasn't much time left on the clock. It appeared the other team would surely be the victor. But then, out of left field, there was a player who knew that his desire to win was greater than his willingness to sustain a loss. This could be the quarterback, a linebacker, or a running back who knew that the "fat lady had not yet sung." It was as if there was a spark plug that was sitting dormant in the engine that all of sudden got fired up, said, "The game is not yet over," and got the motor running again.

My husband and I have spent many years encouraging couples, regardless of age, especially as they contemplated marriage, and stole from an unknown author the quote, "Divorce is not an option." We touted this phrase for a long time and waved the banner, but now must acknowledge that this is not necessarily true. Divorce *is* an option. Marriage or a committed relationship is a choice that a person has made, and a person should be given the choice to decide if they want to remain or leave. There are valid reasons that a player leaves a team, but then there can also be reasons that are more about self-gain. Self-promotion benefits its originator. Team players promote the best for the good of the team. There are some outstanding individual players in all arenas of sports, but the ones who have exhibited the best of a team concept are the players that we herald, cherish, and remember.

The option is yours, but either way, when you step back for a moment to examine your motives, it is when the good of the team is paramount that the right decision will be made for the right reasons. Many allies will alienate you, but you are the one who will ultimately have to live with the decision that was made, as well as the consequences.

The culture of committed relationships and marriage is evolving in our rapidly changing society. What were once sacred mores are no longer viewed as precious, but rather archaic. This has no bearing upon anyone's religious conviction, but transcends every ethnic, racial, economic, or spiritual background.

There is no secret formula to relationships or marriage. Many books will capture one's attention by baiting them with an unwritten promise that they have discovered the plutonium of having a successful relationship. When individuals who purchase and read such books try to apply only one aspect of what they perceive as the secret formula to their relationship, they can become discouraged because they thought it would be only that one item that would forever improve their relationship. It takes time, application and a comprehensive approach for anything to be effective on a long term basis.

A winning sports team wins because they share the common goal of winning, and they love the people on their team. It's the type of love that gives instant respect to another player, even if you disagree with a play they make. It's the type of love that is able to see past the immediate to look at the last few minutes on the clock and believe in your heart that as a team, you can still win. It's that type of love that weathers the arguments in the locker room, playing the blame game, but realizes that the ultimate prize is winning a championship in which they all share in the spoils. Love is about winning, even when you have to lose your ego.

"Love is patient, love is kind. It does not envy, it does not boast, it is not proud. It does not dishonor others, it is not self-seeking, it is not easily angered, it keeps no record of wrongs. Love does not delight in evil, but rejoices with the truth. It always protects, always trusts, always hopes, always perseveres. Love never fails." — 1 Corinthians 13 (NIV)

We have been married for over 40 years and we dated for six years prior to that, and even to this day, we are still learning more about each other as our lives continue to evolve with the variables that affect us as a couple. For over 35 years, we have been working with couples (seriously dating, engaged, and married) and have learned more about ourselves, as well as helping others to explore, discover, and resolve issues that were clogging the pores of their relationships. We don't have a secret formula either, as our marriage began on a great note, got rocky, got better, got rocky again, and now it appears that we are in an even stride of success. We are confident that we love each other today more than we could ever imagine we would after sharing the same marriage bed for over 43 years.

We had pondered for a long time about sharing our years of experience and knowledge on how to help couples, because the basic premise of humility under which both of us operate would often make us wonder in the midst of our own struggles, *What could* we *possibly share with people?* A very dear, trusted friend sat us down, challenged us to take an introspective look at ourselves, and said that the best thing that we could continue to do was to be transparent with all the couples and individuals we talk to. Too often, authors feel compelled to share their success stories but are reticent to expose their vulnerabilities, failures, and where they just screwed up. So with that charge given to us by our friend, we decided to embark upon writing this, a task that has spanned a number of years. But there has always been a gnawing at our guts to get this out, so that those who could benefit from it will pick it up, read it, absorb it, and apply it.

People will purchase home gym equipment with the intent of becoming more fit, and will sometimes experience peer pressure to look better. What typically happens is that the expensive equipment is purchased, and then it begins to gather dust because applying the healthy principles of building a routine is ignored. Rather than trying to look better for others, true change should be for one's internal and external satisfaction, so that you will be pleased with the results, and so that the exercise program fits you and allows you to become consistent with an effective program. The same regimen of consistency is required in building the muscles of a healthy long-term relationship.

Recovering the Fumble

Sometimes you may drop the ball, but that doesn't mean that you let anything stand in the way of a healthy and happy relationship. At times, it may seem that the idea of just walking away is more convenient than staying in the fight to win. I've been there, we've been there, and I'm sure that you have been there as well. So what makes some survive while others seem to fade into the abyss of relationship oblivion? It's that a goal has been clearly set, a mindset has been created, to say that "I'm in it to win it," and to create a plan to get back on track.

Every good running back or quarterback has fumbled the ball, which means that they lost control of it before being tackled. This can be a result of not timing their running stride carefully enough, or not calculating the trajectory of the ball quickly enough, causing it to roll off their fingers, or sometimes even just touching it with the tips of their fingers. When we don't have a good grasp on something, it is easy for it to slip out of our hands and can discourage us, especially when the clock is ticking and we've not scored enough points in our favor. A fumble does not mark the end of the game, but is a simple reminder that one must pay attention to all of the factors of the game and understand how important timing is to any effective play.

Have you ever fumbled the ball in your relationship? This is not even a fair question to ask, because if anyone answers no, then they're not operating in the realm of reality. Alexander Pope said, "To err is human, to forgive, divine." A mistake is just that, a mistake. It is not necessarily an intentional point of sabotage, but rather a point from which one can learn. Although the topic of forgiveness is a book unto itself, it is important to stress that sincere forgiveness is not allowing yourself to be seen as a doormat to be tread upon, but rather a door that opens the opportunity for a new beginning.

Think of how many mistakes you've made personally within the past week. Now multiply that times the number of years that you have lived, and you will see that that number is pretty significant when you put it in numerical terms.

Remember from the beginning of the book I was new to the game of football. As I was learning more about the game, I became a fan of the Seattle Seahawks. But let's not forget I am a resident of Chicago; I also support my own home team the Chicago Bears.

One of the most talked about fourth-quarter comebacks, Bears vs Eagles in 2007. The Bears trailed 16-12 and had not scored a touchdown at their own 3-yard line with 1:52 minutes to play and no timeouts remaining. Despite the odds, focused on winning, with confidence, working together and using the skills of their players the Bears won the game.

If every professional sports team that we knew of focused on the failures of its players rather than their potential, there would be more cuts and trades in the middle of a season. However, there is a tenacity that a good coach has to have to continue to be observant, provide good feedback, chastise when necessary, and lead the players in the direction they should go. Good relationships may not be easy, but they sure are worth it! Hang in there; you just scored a Love Touchdown.

MARRIAGE PLAYBOOK
COACHING STRATEGY
Fourth QTR: Winning the Game

- Refuse to allow divorce to be a topic of conversation in your home. If your spouse knows that come hell or high water, you will never leave them and vice versa, both of you will go about the business of out-loving, out-caring, and out-hugging the other.

- Share your successes and the struggles of your relationship. It will help to encourage and challenge another couple, while at the same time giving you an appreciative perspective of your own marriage.

- Don't take each other for granted. Use common sense to recognize that the grass may not be greener on the other side.

- Rid yourselves of negative influences (people and/or couples) who drain the life out of you and your marriage, rather than pouring the water of life into it.

Your Love Touchdown Playlist

Take a look at these plays to find out how to love your husband and how to make him happy; then place a checkmark next to one of the plays that you will commit to making today.

- Spend an entire day anticipating his wants.
- Invite his friends over for dinner.
- Sit on his lap.
- Book a hotel getaway for no reason.
- Play some music and dance together in the living room.
- Spend the day doing whatever he wants.

2 minute wrap-up

What are some of the key points that you have learned from this section?

_____

_____

_____

What type of playbook strategy would you develop to improve or keep your relationship consistent?

_____

_____

_____

If you were providing advice to a friend based on what you read in this section, what would be the one key takeaway?

_____

_____

_____

EPILOGUE

It has been a labor of love for us to work together to write this book for those on the path of trying to stay in committed relationships. This is a collection of painful truths that we had to deal with in our own marriage. At times, we were too arrogant, stubborn, or just plain ignorant to seek out the assistance of wise counsel that would have helped us avoid painful pitfalls in our marriage.

After four decades we have known and been married to each other, we will truly admit that we are not the same people who started out on this journey together. We also realize that we have become better people as a result of that journey. Our fruits of the spirit have been tested and tried, and there were seasons when it seemed as though the fruit on the vine was dead and would definitely not yield a productive harvest.

We are grateful to those who stood with us in our public victories and our private shames but have kept us accountable and committed. Tears and fears have plagued our home many times, but at the end of the day, we have always said that it is better to stick it out with this one than to have to corral a new horse and tame it. As the old joke goes, a woman was asked if she ever considered dumping her husband and marrying another, to which she promptly replied, "Are you crazy? It took me forever to train this one!"

LOVE TOUCHDOWN!

One of our favorite authors is Gary Chapman, who is well-known for his many writings on relationships. Most known for his book titled *The Five Love Languages*, we believe that Gary is correct when he discusses the importance of understanding the emotional language of your partner. If you've engaged in conversations with either men or women, their language is dominated by what they love. Shopping, golf, baseball, food, and other topics are dear to them, and when you speak their language, they pay attention to you more and enjoy being around you. We have chosen football, as it is a favorite topic that dominates conversations from the early fall to early winter.

In this book, we used football to create a playbook that parallels the building blocks of relationships. This book was designed to help you increase your knowledge of this passionate American sport, while at the same time giving you tips on how to improve your marriage. Imagine how much closer your spouse will draw to your heart when he sees you attempting to understand his favorite pastime. When you learn to accept his fanaticism and appreciate his love of the game, you will draw closer to him than you ever dreamed possible. So, no matter what stage of a relationship you find yourself in, using the tools from this playbook will help you increase your marriage bliss and develop a deeper level of companionship with your spouse. It will also help you understand his fascination with the game of football, and whenever the mood is right, it will give you the techniques you need to score a Love Touchdown.

MARRIAGE PLAYBOOK
Football Glossary

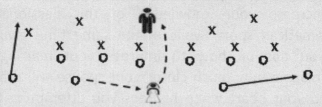

- Blitz: act of charging directly for the passer as soon as the ball is snapped.

- Bomb: a long forward pass, especially one to a teammate who scores a touchdown.

- Center: handles the ball on every play and snaps the ball to the holder.

- First down: a team has the ability to run 4 plays in order to advance the ball 10 yards. A gain of 10 yards results in a first down; thereby allowing the team to retain possession of the ball.

- Free Agent: an athlete who is not under contract and is free to auction off his or her services and sign a contract with the team that offers the most money.

- Fumble: to fail to hold the ball after having touched it and carried it.

- Handoff: an offensive play in which a player

hands the ball to a teammate.

- Holder: the person who is to catch and place the football for the kicker.

- Huddle: to gather in a close mass to discuss ideas and to make a decision.

- Incompletion: a ball not caught by the intended receiver.

- Interception: a pass that is caught by a defensive player and thus stolen from the offense.

- Key On: watches the position and movements of an opponent in order to anticipate a play.

- Linebacker: a defensive football player. The linebacker's job is to defend the goal area of the football field and to block plays by opposing team.

- Line of Scrimmage: the imaginary line separating the teams at the beginning of a play.

- Offside: illegally crossing the line of scrimmage in advance of the ball being hiked at the beginning of a play.

- Possession: having control of the ball.

- Quarterback: a back who usually lines up directly behind the center and directs the offense of the game.

- Running back: the running back has one of the toughest jobs on the football field as they have a responsibility on every offensive play. Like the quarterback, they must know every play. The running back will also make physical contact on virtually every down during the team's offensive possession.

- Rushing: to carry the ball on a running play.

- Substitution: the act of a player running onto the playing field to replace another.

- Tackle: the act of seizing, grasping, or bringing the opponent down to the ground.

- Touchdown: a score that is worth 6 points when a team goes across the opposite team's goal line.

- Turnover: loss of the ball via a fumble or interception.

- Two-Minute Warning: a time-out called by an official to notify both teams that two minutes remain in the half.

- Wide receiver: an offensive player. The wide receiver is one of the fastest players on the field alongside of cornerback and running back. When the ball is thrown by the quarterback, the wide receiver's job is to catch it and try to score a touchdown.

THANK YOU!

Thanks for supporting us with your own copy of Love Touchdown. We hope that, whether you are dating, newly married, or a veteran of marriage, you find some new strategies you can adopt to make your relationship or marriage stronger. Our labor of love is borne out of tears, disappointments, good and bad lessons, but most of all, commitment.

Made in the USA
Coppell, TX
06 February 2022